Dinosaur
Puzzles
for the Scroll Saw

by Judy & Dave Peterson

Fox
Chapel Publishing Co. Inc.
1970 Broad Street • East Petersburg, PA 17520 • www.foxchapelpublishing.com

Acknowledgments

A note of thanks to the Spielmans and all the other designers on whose patterns I practiced cutting.

© 2002 Fox Chapel Publishing Company, Inc.

Dinosaur Puzzles for the Scroll Saw is an original work, first published in 2002 by Fox Chapel Publishing Company, Inc. The patterns contained herein are copyrighted by the author. Artists purchasing this book have permission to make up to 3 photocopies of each individual pattern for personal use only. The patterns themselves are not to be duplicated for resale or distribution under any circumstances.

Publisher:	Alan Giagnocavo
Project Editor:	Ayleen Stellhorn
Layout and Design:	Linda Eberly
Cover Design:	Keren Holl
Interior Photography:	Keren Holl

ISBN # 1–56523–184–8
Library of Congress Preassigned Card Number: 2002102622

To order your copy of this book,
please send check or money order
for the cover price plus $3.00 shipping to:
Fox Books
1970 Broad Street
East Petersburg, PA 17520

Or visit us on the web at
www.foxchapelpublishing.com

Manufactured in Korea

Table of Contents

About the Authors

Judy Peterson

A former school teacher and librarian, Judy found her niche in life as a woodworker. She bought her first saw in 1990 and within the first six months was cutting and creating her own designs. She now sells her puzzles at art and craft shows around the country. A winner of many prizes, Judy was featured in the December 1997 issue of *Wisconsin Trails*. Most recently, her article on another of her puzzles was published in the Spring issue of *Scroll Saw Workshop* magazine. She teaches scroll sawing for the Woodcraft store in her home town of Madison, Wisconsin, and in her spare time, she reads, keeps track of politics on TV, gardens, cooks, turns bowls on her lathe and puts together other people's flat puzzles.

Dave Peterson

Dave is a Senior Systems Analyst for a small mail order company. His interest in computers, data bases and spreadsheets makes him suited to run the record-keeping side of Judy's small business, called Fan Taminals. Add a digital camera, a flair for writing and a little organizational skill into the mix, and out comes this book. In his spare time, he reads, is active in the local Macintosh Users' Group and tries to keep up with his wife.

Judy and Dave can be reached via e-mail at FanTamdsp@aol.com.

Introduction

Why puzzles?

I like puzzles! These days when I'm not making my own puzzles, I'm likely to be doing someone else's. In 1989 my family and I made our annual trek to a nearby Renaissance Faire. As a souvenir I bought a five-piece rabbit puzzle. While it was attractive, it was not interlocking, so you really couldn't handle it.

The first thing I cut out when I brought home my first scroll saw—a wonderful new toy—was a three-piece rabbit. When I began designing my own puzzles, I decided all of them would be interlocking. The puzzles in this book reflect that decision I made in 1990: all of these puzzles are interlocking. That means that once you have them in a standing position you can pick them up by any piece and turn them completely around without having them fall apart (but use caution with the Maiasaura). You can, that is, as long as you don't tip them!

All of the puzzles in this book are interlocking. The puzzle pieces stay together when you pick up an assembled puzzle.

Why Dinos?

I discovered at age 50 that I liked dinosaurs again. I had already designed quite a few puzzles and decided to try my hand at dinosaurs. While this book contains 30 patterns, there are only 24 different dinosaur species represented. That's because I do more than one version of the better-known dinos. For example, there are three Tyrannosaurus Rex patterns (the Toy Rex, the 6-piece version, plus the one which appears in a puzzle titled "In the Cretaceous," the largest puzzle in the book).

How complicated should a puzzle be for a preschooler? This question is important to someone who makes puzzles for a living. It's important to someone who's making a puzzle for a child, too. The rule of thumb I use is "age plus one piece." This varies with the child. The more dexterous the child, and/or the more experience the child has with puzzles, the more complicated the puzzle can be.

Many of the dinosaurs in this book are not well known. That's why we've included a little information about each one on the patterns. This is intended to level the playing field for those of you who are making one or more of these puzzles for a child. Chances are good the child will already know about most of them.

Why hardwoods?

When I was starting with my scroll saw, I tried cutting many different types of wood. I found I got much less "chip-out" using hardwoods. Hardwoods seem to be more uniformly dense. Another natural advantage of hardwoods is that they come in different colors, and so they don't need to be painted. Moreover, hardwoods look good with an oil finish.

When the idea of trying to sell my puzzles occurred to me, I tried painting them, but that took forever. Besides, I'm really not good at painting. I'm much better with a saw. This is the reason I cut the eyes, the mouth and other details.

I have also found hardwoods to be very durable. Puzzles cut from hardwoods will stand up to a lot of use, which is important whether you are cutting a puzzle for a young child or an "old" child.

Getting Started

Safety First

It should come as no surprise that cutting thick wood generates a lot of sawdust. Breathing sawdust is not good for you. In my workshop, I have a dust collector and an air cleaner. The dust collector picks up the large particles and a lot of the small ones. The air cleaner is mounted on the ceiling and removes a high percentage of the particles the dust collector misses. However, the air in the workshop will still have lots of tiny particles floating around. To ensure that I'm breathing clean air, I wear a dust mask that uses replaceable filters. I strongly suggest you do the same.

Dust that accumulates on your piece as you work is also a safety hazard. You'll do a better job of cutting and be safer if your saw has a good dust blower. Allowing the dust blower to blow dust away from your cut line is much safer than trying to brush the dust away with your hand.

Eye protection is a must! I use my regular glasses, however, I have Titanium frames and hardened lenses. When I'm sanding, I wear side shields. These translucent plastic devices slide onto your frames and keep flying particles from hitting your eyes from the side. Whatever kind of eye protection you use in your workshop should include side shielding. If you don't need prescription lenses, use safety goggles.

Lighting is important, too. Make sure you have enough light in your workshop so you can see what you're doing. I have two swing arm lamps mounted on my saw. These lamps come with clamps, and you can usually find somewhere to attach them if you don't have a mount for them on your saw. I find that I can cut longer with light coming from both sides. This eliminates shadows and lots of eye strain.

I also wear a hearing protector. If you're into serious woodworking, you would be well advised to at least invest in a mask, eye protection, some type of hearing protection and a dust collector.

Many finishes, including Danish oil, which I suggest for finishing the dinosaur puzzles, have dangerous fumes.

It is important to do your finishing in a well-ventilated area. It is equally important to let the paper towels or rags dry thoroughly before discarding them. Never put them in a closed container or closed garbage bag before they are thoroughly dry.

Choosing a board

If your intent is to cut only one puzzle from a board, you need only to choose a board wide enough and long enough to fit the puzzle. If you want to cut more than one puzzle from a board, choose a board wide enough to fit the largest puzzle.

You'll see references in this book to 4/4 hardwood. (When you speak it, say "four quarter.") When a board is cut from a log, it is sized by the quarter inch. Usually by the time it appears in a rack at a lumberyard, a 4/4 board has been planed to $^{13}/_{16}$-inch thick.

Because my puzzles are all designed to stand, the wider the board is, the more stable the puzzles will be. I usually use boards that are $^{15}/_{16}$-inch thick. I don't recommend using boards less than ¾ inch thick.

Choosing a blade

I recommend a #7 or #7 reverse tooth blade to cut 4/4 hardwoods. The kerf is wide enough to allow the pieces to slide in and out easily. At the same time, the puzzles will hang together well. When using a thicker board, use a #9 blade. Use a #5 blade for a board less than ¾-inch thick.

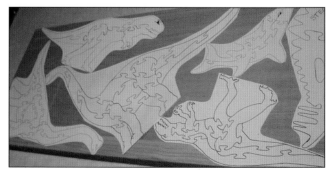

Careful planning will allow you to cut many dinosaur puzzles from one board.

Laying out patterns

For best results, you should plan how you're going to lay puzzle patterns out on a board before you start to glue them down. Trim around each pattern, trimming closest to the tails, noses and feet—any part that is likely to be closest to other patterns or to the edge of the board.

Wood boards can be very dynamic. You'll often find wavy grains and color changes. Be sure to take advantage of these natural features. Wood boards can also contain flaws. Position your patterns carefully to avoid cracks and knots.

Use a spray adhesive to attach your patterns to the wood. Choose a product that mentions "repositionable bonding" on the label. Spray the back of the pattern, not the board.

Using plastic tape

Many of the hardwoods are so dense or have so much resin that the blade stays in one place long enough to cause the wood to burn. If you're planning to cut a light-colored hardwood, be sure to glue the pattern down and then cover it with 2-inch clear

Clear packing tape makes cutting easier.

packing tape. Any brand will do, but don't purchase a product with Mylar threads.

This is my interpretation of what happens: The heat provided by the blade melts some of the plastic. The liquid plastic provides lubrication for the blade. In addition to reducing or eliminating burning, it is easier to push the blade through the wood.

I recommend using clear packing tape when cutting cherry, maple and birch boards, as well as any light-colored exotics. Tape walnut if it is thicker than $^{15}/_{16}$ inch.

Cutting on the line

Cutting on the line is fairly important on the outer edges of the puzzle. It's very important for facial features and somewhat important on the inner cuts.

If you wobble on the outside edge of a puzzle, you can either re-cut it or ignore it. If you get off the line on the feature cuts, stop cutting. Look where you are and see if the cut can be saved. If it can, try to do so. If it can't, throw the puzzle out and try again.

On the interior, or interlocking, cuts, accuracy is not terribly important. What is important is the shape of the key. In order for the key to remain in the keyhole, the head of the key must be larger than the neck of the key. It also must be balanced so that there is material on both sides of the neck.

GOOD vs. BAD KEY DESIGN

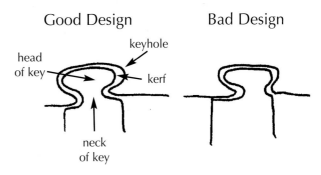

On puzzles with large pieces, there is a lot of room for error. The smaller and more complex the pieces, the more important accuracy becomes.

Keys (the little knobs that hold the puzzle together) can be a variety of shapes.

Sanding

I do a lot of sanding because my puzzles are meant to be handled. Smooth feels better. In the wooden puzzle art show booth, "smooth" means "sales." For the best effect, all the surfaces of these puzzles should be sanded. In addition, round off the sharp corners to avoid injury to those who handle them.

Cutting Dino Features

Almost all of my puzzles represent some kind of life form, real or imaginary. Thus, most of them have facial features. For the first three or four years after I started my business, I drew those features on the puzzles. I didn't feel I was very good at it. I could never seem to get the eyes the same on both sides of the same puzzle or correct in relation to one another.

Then a light dawned: A friend suggested that I cut the features with the saw.

I developed a variety of eye shapes and re-did all of the applicable patterns, incorporating the facial features into each. I find it much easier to cut them than to draw them, and the effect is much better. Of the puzzles in this book, six need drilled eyes; the rest have cut eyes.

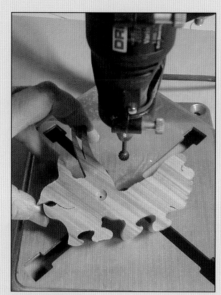

Drilling Eyes: Drill a hole in the center of the eye with the drill bit before cutting the pattern. The eye socket should be created after the pattern has been scrolled. Put a ¼-inch burr in a rotary power tool, position the head piece so the drilled hole is in the center of the eye, then carve out the eye socket.

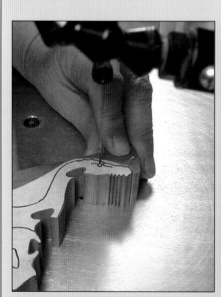
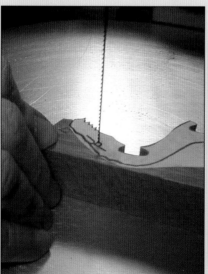
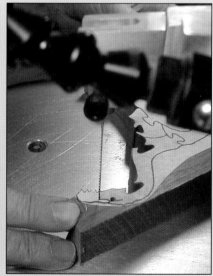

Cutting Eyes: Make an access cut with the saw. From there, follow the lines on the pattern. If the eye is a simple hole—round, square, diamond or half circle—just cut it with the saw. Some of the animals have eyebrow cuts. To make these, cut the eye hole first, then back out or turn around and cut the eyebrow.

I use a drum sander and a belt sander with a disk sander built in. If you don't have a drum sander, don't run out to buy one just to make the puzzles in this book. I use all this equipment because my business is designing and making puzzles. All the flat sanding can be done with a disk pad chucked into a drill. It will be helpful if you have a drill with a variable speed lock.

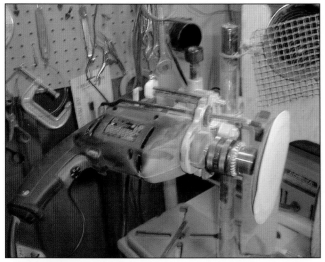

A disk pad chucked into a drill with a variable speed lock is ideal for quick flat sanding.

Finishing

Hardwood puzzles look great with an oil finish. In addition, Danish oil has three important advantages. First, it is absorbed by the wood and therefore creates no build-up that can affect how the pieces fit together. Second, it cures in about 30 days, by which time it has polymerized. This strengthens the puzzles and makes them "waterproof." (Basically, if they get wet, the water will not raise the grain.) Third, it's non-toxic after it has dried. This is an important characteristic if the puzzle is to be given to a child.

Danish oil comes in an assortment of hues. Because I want to enhance, not obscure, the natural color of the hardwoods, I use a clear Danish oil.

I do not recommend brushing a finish on the puzzle pieces because the build up may affect the fit of the pieces. After some experimentation, I have discovered that immersion works best. I pour oil into the bag, then insert the puzzle pieces, one at a time. I dip the pieces briefly, then stand them on a flat, non-oil-absorbing surface covered with paper towels.

Using a Drum Sander

I estimate that using a drum sander reduces my flat sanding time by 75 percent. The price I pay is that I occasionally crunch a puzzle. I keep track of which patterns cause such problems and simply don't use a drum sander for those puzzles. For the patterns in this book, I have found it safe to use a drum sander on all of the puzzles except for the following: Allosaur, Cryolophosaur, Oviraptor and Velociraptor. Practice on puzzles with large long pieces, like the Apatosaur. Be very careful with the Brachiosaurus and the Barosaurus. You may want to remove the tails before you begin.

1. Put a #64 rubber band completely around the outside of the puzzle.
2. Group the puzzles you have according to the thickness of the wood.
3. Start with the group made of the thickest wood. Position each puzzle on the conveyor belt so it goes through with the grain.
4. Run the first group through on both sides. Use one or more push sticks to support each puzzle as it goes through.
5. Adjust the height of the sanding drum down for the next group.

As necessary, I wipe the excess oil off with paper towels. The more cut line details there are in a puzzle, the more attention it needs at this step. After drying any pieces that need it, I reassemble the puzzle and let it air-dry overnight.

If you choose to paint a puzzle, seal the wood then use acrylic craft paints. Don't paint the cut edges on the inside of the puzzle.

Pattern Classifications

The patterns in this book cover a wide variety of skill levels, both for the puzzle maker and the puzzle receiver.

Easy Puzzles: A linear puzzle is one that has all its pieces in a line. Each piece connects only to the next one. The shape of each key is a geometric design meant to be easier for young children to match.

Toys: These are the shapes that I think of as "Stuffed Animal" puzzles. They are the kind of dinosaurs that appear on Saturday morning cartoons. They're not realistic, but they are very popular with two and three-year-olds. These are definitely starter puzzles for the child and practice pieces for those of you who are beginning scrollers.

Realistic puzzles are much the same as the toys, except they have more realistic shapes.

Intermediate Puzzles: Unlike the linear puzzles, each of these has pieces that connect to more than one other piece. They are more difficult to put together. The child has to see all the connections and be able to line them up so that all the keys will drop into the appropriate keyholes. The four intermediate puzzles in this book were designed for children ages four and five. All of the pieces are large, less likely to get lost and harder to break.

Advanced Puzzles: These puzzles are medium to hard to put together and to cut. Most of them have small pieces that could easily be swallowed. Do not give these puzzles to small children and do not leave them where small children might find them.

Dioramas: These puzzle scenes include several dinosaur subjects and some landscape elements. They are more difficult to put together. They also require some tight, intricate cutting and some special cutting techniques.

Claws and Teeth

Claws and teeth in my puzzles are exaggerated in size. Claws need to be thick enough to withstand sanding and play. The Velociraptor claws, both hand and foot, are the most fragile, so I chose that dinosaur for the pictures to illustrate the exaggerations.

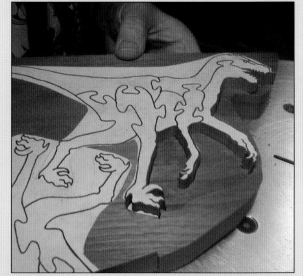
Claws 2

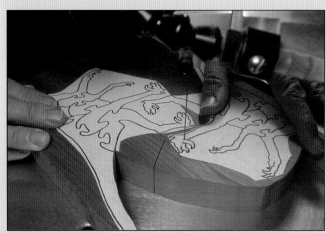
Claws 1

▲ I generally start at the back foot and cut the claws on both feet. Then I cut around to the arms, complete them, then go up to the jaws and cut the teeth. At that point, I cut both the bottom jaw/arm piece and the other arm free. These are the most fragile pieces. Set them aside. Now cut the face around to the eye detail and finish up.

To cut the teeth, start at the front of the bottom jaw. Cut up to the point of the first tooth. Then pivot to go down and then up to the point of the next tooth. This is easier said than done, and you will need to practice. The trick is to stop pushing forward as you pivot. ▶

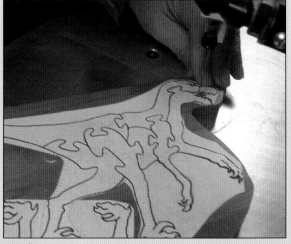
Teeth

Cutting a Triceratops Puzzle

Tools and Supplies

Scroll saw with dust
   blower
Belt sander
Plain or reverse tooth
   blades (#5, #7, #9)
Spray adhesive
Square
Clear 2" packing tape
Disk pad
Drill
Drill stand

Flap sander
Flat trays
Glue box
Metal tray
Paper towels
Pile of rags
Plastic bags, gallon
   resealable
Rubber gloves
Rubber finger tips
Sanding disks

I chose a redgum board, 48" x 8⅜" x ⅞", for the Triceratops puzzle in the following demonstration. A little bit of planning and some trimming of the patterns allowed me to cut 10 puzzles from that board: 6-piece Triceratops, Microceratops, Monoclonius, Toy Bronto, 6-piece Apatosaur, Pachyrhinosaur, Protoceratops, 12-piece Apatosaur, Toy Rex and Mussaurus.

When you have chosen the board you plan to use for your Triceratops puzzle, trim the pattern and use a spray adhesive to attach the pattern to the board. If you have chosen a very dense hardwood—like cherry, maple or birch—tape the pattern down with 2-inch clear packing tape (the kind without Mylar threads). The tape seems to act as a lubricant for the blade and minimizes any potential burning.

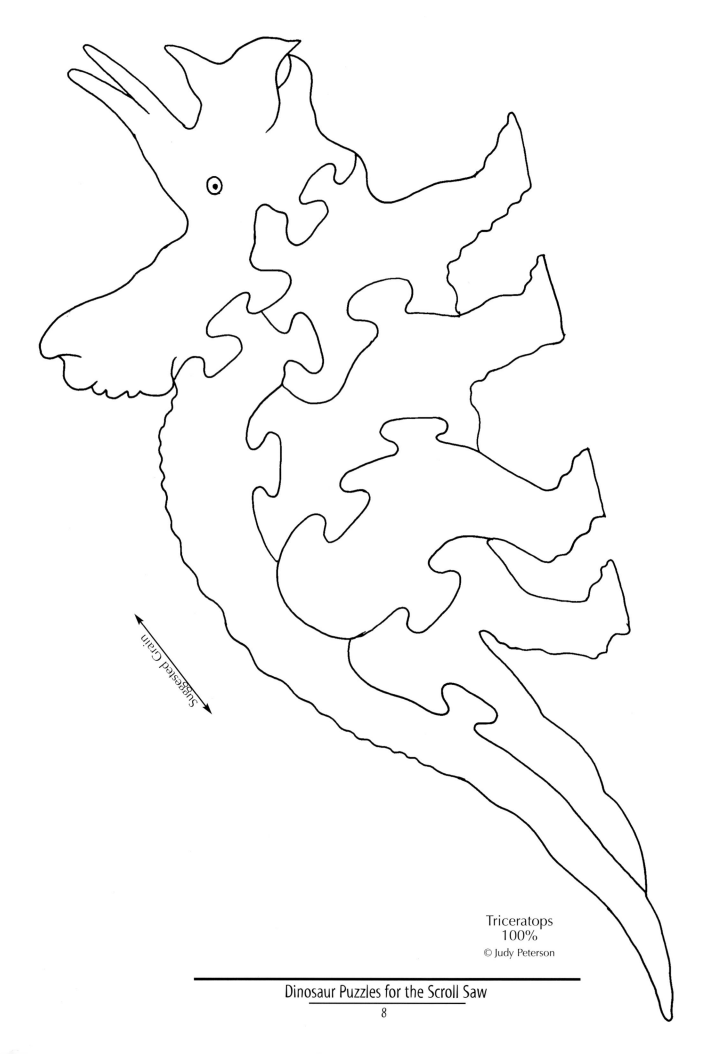

Triceratops
100%
© Judy Peterson

Suggested Grain

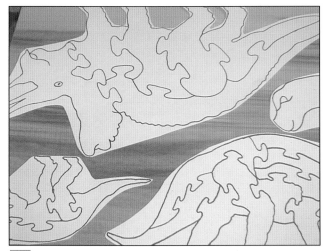

1 Multiple puzzles can be cut from one board. I positioned the triceratops so that the white streak in this redgum board would give him white feet and a white tail. The arrows on the patterns show grain direction. You won't always have a board that allows the best placement; try to come close.

2 Cut the dinos apart so you have smaller pieces with which to work. I try to cut out as much of the items as possible as I'm passing by. In the case of the Triceratops, that means cutting along the baseline of the toy Bronto, then along the backbone of the Monoclonius, and finally along the baseline of the Microceratops.

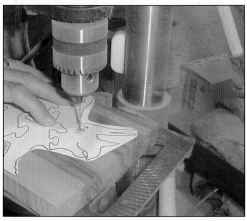

3 Now that the Triceratops is on a piece of redgum all to itself, drill the hole in the center of the eye. In this photo, I am using a 1/16-inch drill bit.

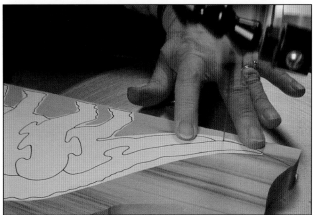

4 Start to cut the Triceratops puzzle at the tip of the tail. If you find that the paper pattern lifts off the board as you saw, position your fingers as shown or tape the pattern down with a piece of clear plastic packing tape.

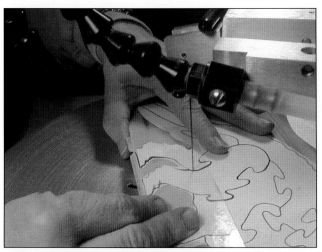

5 Continue to cut the outline around the bottom of the tail and the two hind legs. Cut around the forward hind leg piece as shown in the photograph.

6 Remove the leg piece from your work, peel the pattern off and set this piece safely aside.

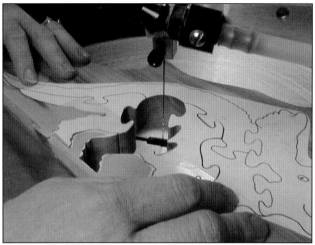

7 | Moving toward the head, cut out the next piece. **TIP:** As you remove each piece, interlock it with the pieces you cut earlier. This will give you a chance to verify that the blade is vertical and that the pieces fit correctly.

8 | Proceed to cut around the bottom of the front leg. Cut all the way up to the bottom tip of the beak, as indicated by the arrow in the photograph, then stop.

9 | Pull the blade back slightly and turn to the right into the scrap wood. Turn the piece so that you approach the tip of the beak from what would be the front.

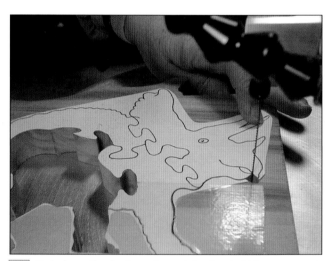

10 | Cut along the bottom line of the beak. When you get to the point where the tip of the bottom jaw meets the top jaw, you have created a small piece of scrap. Stop the saw and remove that piece of wood.

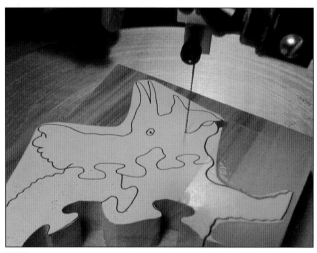

11 | Back the blade out of the cut you've just made. Reposition the blade so you are able to make a clean approach to the lower jaw line.

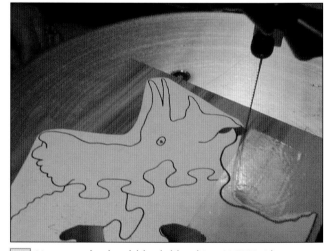

12 | Your puzzle should look like this. **NOTE:** Always stop and remove those small bits of scrap. If you don't, they'll invariably catch on something and hang up.

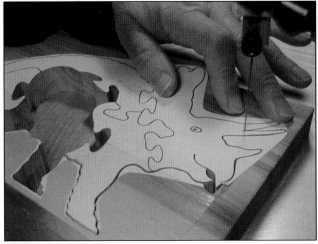

13 Starting at the tip of the beak, cut around the nose horn and up around the first horn on the head. From there, cut to the bottom of the V. Instead of trying to turn the piece to create a perfect V, follow the next steps.

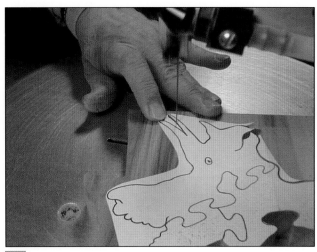

14 Back the blade out halfway to the tip of the horn. Then turn the piece around into the scrap. ("Turning into the scrap" means to turn your wood 180 degrees so the teeth of the blade face into the scrap wood.)

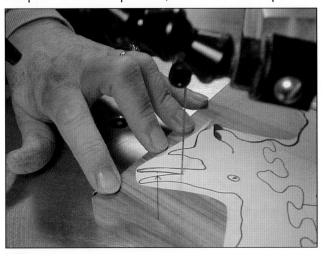

15 Back the blade into the V. You are now positioned to start cutting the second horn. The arrow in this photograph points to the hole in the waste where I turned the blade around.

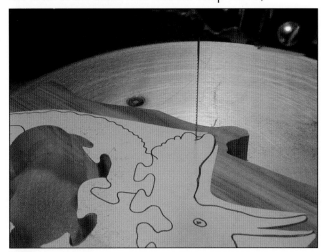

16 Cut around the second horn and proceed to the top of the frill. Stop when you get to the position shown in the photograph.

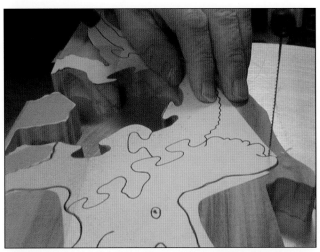

17 Back the blade up slightly and proceed down the back side of the crest, making the detail cuts as you go.

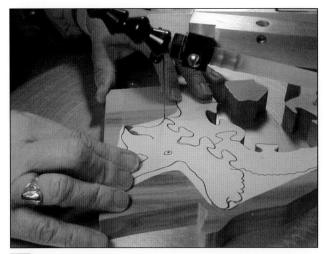

18 Finish cutting out the head and remove it from the saw table.

19 Note that it isn't necessary to follow the line around the outside of the head perfectly. When the pattern has been removed, no one will be any the wiser.

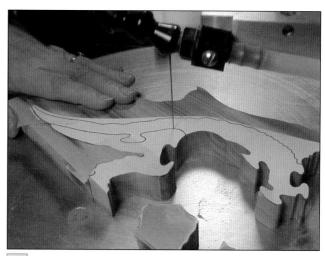

20 Cut out the front leg piece and proceed to separate the hind leg from the backbone piece.

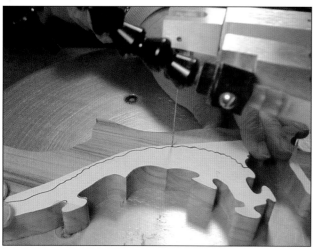

21 Finally, cut out the backbone piece. Notice that there should be plenty of scrap left so you can hold onto the piece safely and securely.

22 Reassemble the cut pieces. If the pattern is stuck to the wood, simply sand it off.

Sanding

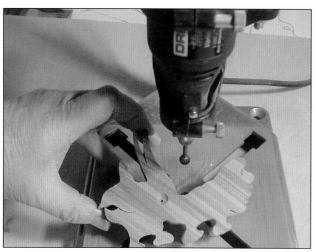

23 Using a rotary power tool with a ¼-inch bur, create the eye socket around the eye hole drilled in Step 3.

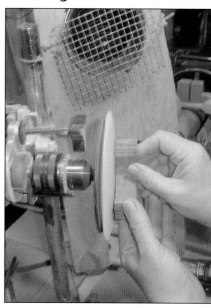

24 The drill stand keeps the working surface at the necessary 90-degree angle and can be adjusted up and down. Chuck the disk pad into the drill and apply a 220-grit adhesive-backed sandpaper disk to it. Hold the piece firmly and lightly sand the front and back surfaces.

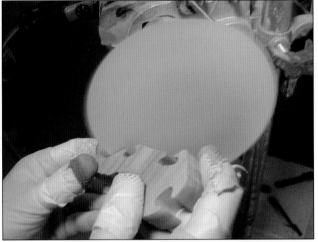

25 When the front and back surfaces are sufficiently smooth, inspect the cut surfaces for any burs. Lightly sand off any wood fibers or other flaws. Sand all the outside cut surfaces smooth to the touch. Sand the interior cuts only enough to remove stray wood fibers.

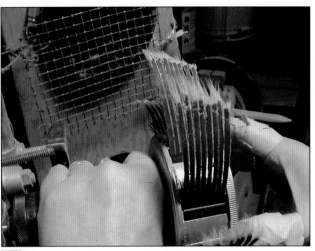

26 This machine is called a flap sander. When it's turned on, the rotating sandpaper will quickly round surface edges. Fingertip protection is absolutely necessary, as you'll see in the next photo.

Finishing

27 Steadily move the piece under the flap sander. Don't hold the piece in one place too long. Your goal is to gently round the edges.

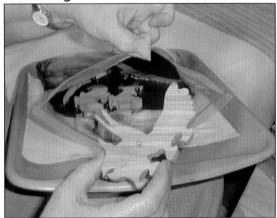

28 Fill a gallon-size resealable plastic bag with clear Danish oil. Place the puzzle, one piece at a time, into the bag.

29 Dip the pieces briefly, remove them from the bag, and stand them on a flat surface covered with paper towels to air dry. **NOTE:** Make sure the flat surface won't absorb excess oil. I use party trays that I found at a local party goods store.

30 Remove any excess oil with a paper towel as needed. The more cut line detail there is in a puzzle piece, the more attention it needs at this step. Reassemble the puzzle and let it dry overnight. (Notice the white feet that resulted from placing the pattern to take advantage of the natural color in the wood.)

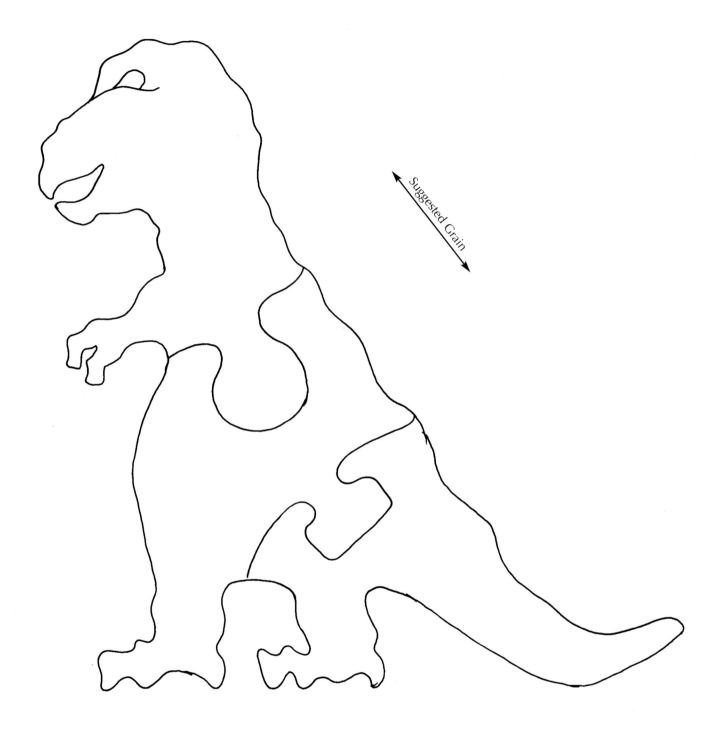

Suggested Grain

Toy Rex
100%
© Judy Peterson

Toy Rex

Easy

Tyrannosaurus Rex (King Tyrant Lizard) is easily one of the scariest dinos of the Cretaceous Age. Oddly enough, he's also a much-loved subject of children. Notice the two geometric cuts.
(Cut from redgum.)

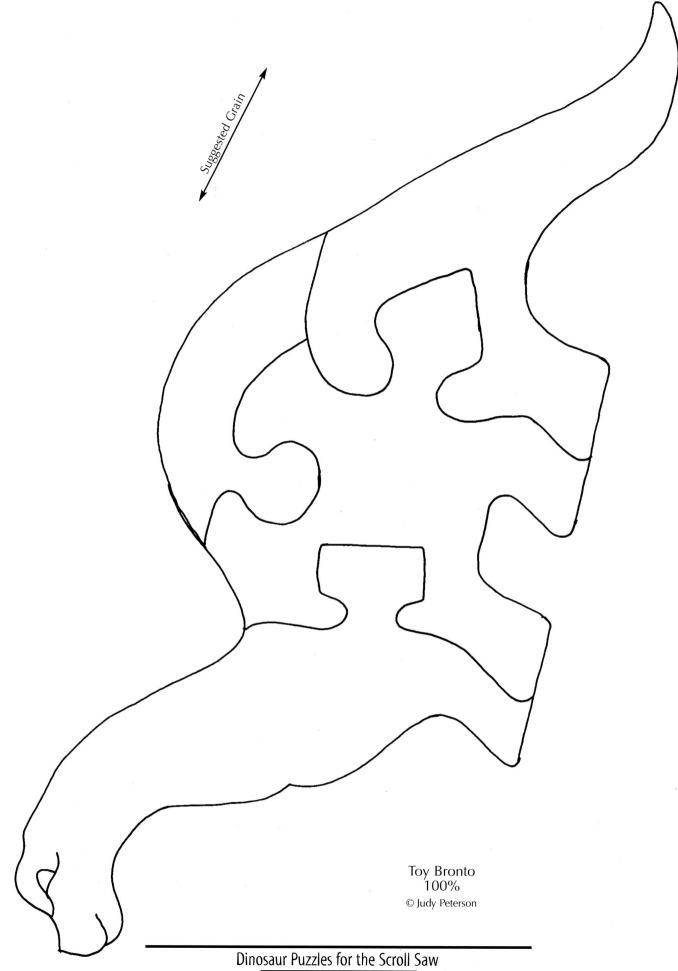

Suggested Grain

Toy Bronto
100%
© Judy Peterson

Toy Bronto

Easy

Brontosaurus was recently renamed Apatosaur (Deceptive Lizard).
Compare this easy version to the advanced puzzle on page 40 to
see how I altered this puzzle for children. (Cut from butternut.)

Suggested Grain

Toy Stego
100%

© Judy Peterson

Dinosaur Puzzles for the Scroll Saw

Toy Stego

The rounded plates, shortened tail spikes and geometric keys make
Stegosaur (Plated Lizard) a fun-shaped dino for young puzzle
lovers. See the advanced realistic Stego puzzle on page 59.
(Cut from butternut.)

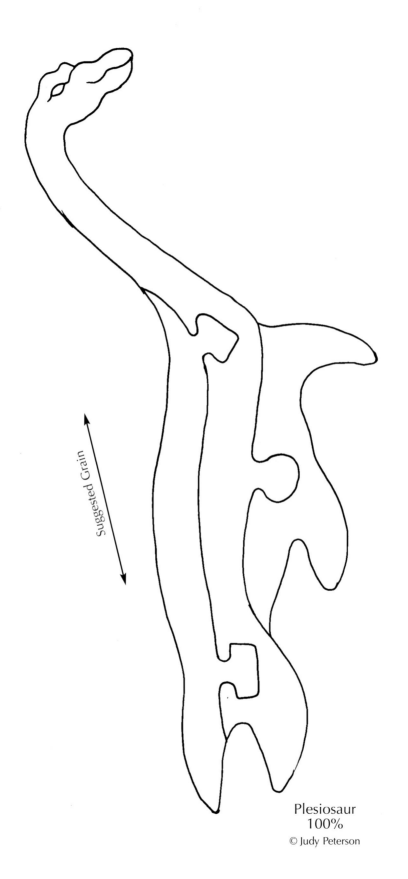

Suggested Grain

Plesiosaur
100%

© Judy Peterson

Plesiosaur

Plesiosaur (Near Lizard) is a marine reptile from the Jurassic Age.
This fish-eater was about 10 feet long and was found world-wide.
(Cut from zebrawood.)

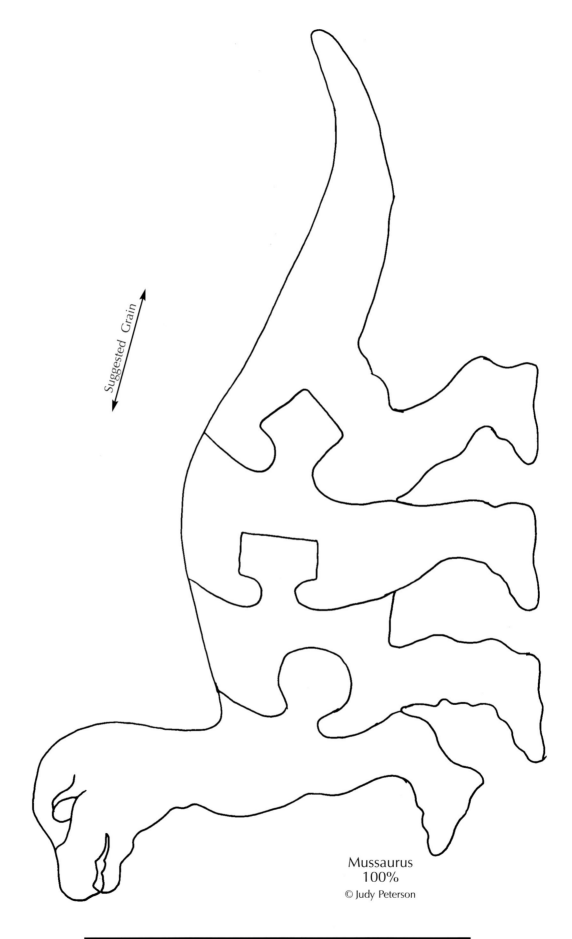

Suggested Grain

Mussaurus
100%

© Judy Peterson

Mussaurus

Easy

Mussaurus (Mouse Lizard) is a plant-eating Prosauropod from the Triassic Age. Its height and weight are unknown because only fossils of juveniles have been found. (Cut from redgum.)

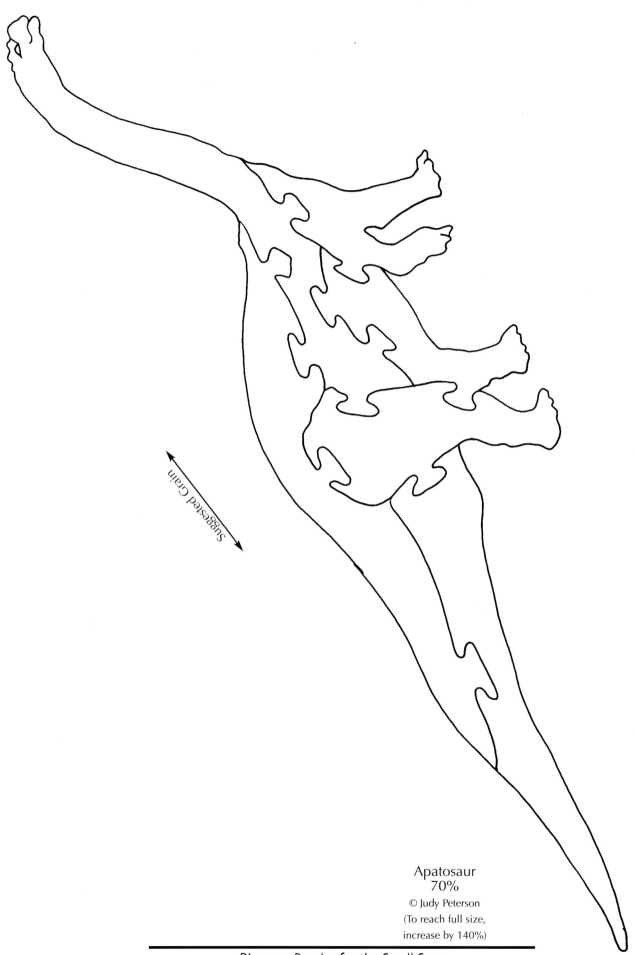

Suggested Grain

Apatosaur
70%

© Judy Peterson

(To reach full size,
increase by 140%)

Dinosaur Puzzles for the Scroll Saw

24

Apatosaur

Apatosaur (Deceptive Lizard) was formerly called Brontosaur.
A Sauropod of the Jurassic Age, this animal was found in North
America and Europe. It ate plants and grew to be about 75 feet
long, 15 feet tall and 30 tons. (Cut from redgum.)

Suggested Grain

Stegosaur
100%

© Judy Peterson

Stegosaur

Intermediate

Stegosaur (Plated Lizard) lived during the Jurassic Age in Europe and North America. It was a plant-eater that grew to be about 25 feet long and 11 feet tall at the hip. (Cut from cherry.)

Suggested Grain

Tyrannosaurus Rex
100%
© Judy Peterson

Dinosaur Puzzles for the Scroll Saw

Tyrannosaurus Rex

Tyrannosaurus Rex (King Tyrant Lizard) needs little introduction. This meat-eating Therapod lived during the Cretaceous Age and was found in North America. It stood about 18 feet tall and was 50 feet long. (Cut from cherry.)

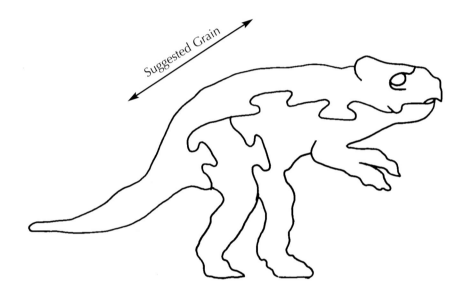

Suggested Grain

Microceratops
100%
© Judy Peterson

Microceratops

Microceratops (Tiny Horned Face) was a Ceratopsian from the Cretaceous Age. Found only in Asia, this tiny plant-eater was a mere 30 inches long. (Cut from walnut.)

Suggested Grain

Monoclonius
100%

© Judy Peterson

Monoclonius

Monoclonius (Single Stem) was found in North America during the Cretaceous Age. This Ceratopsian was a 20-foot-long plant eater. It was one of the first Ceratopsian fossils ever found.
(Cut from redgum.)

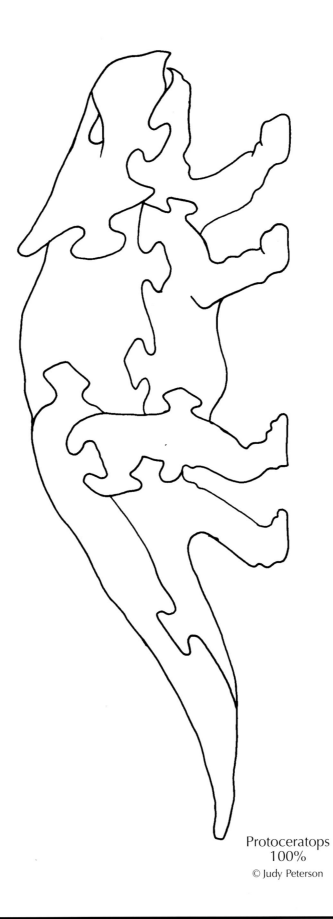

Suggested Grain

Protoceratops
100%

© Judy Peterson

Protoceratops

Protoceratops (First Horned Face) is an early member of the Ceratopsian family. This dinosaur ate plants and lived in Asia during the Cretaceous Age. (Cut from maca.)

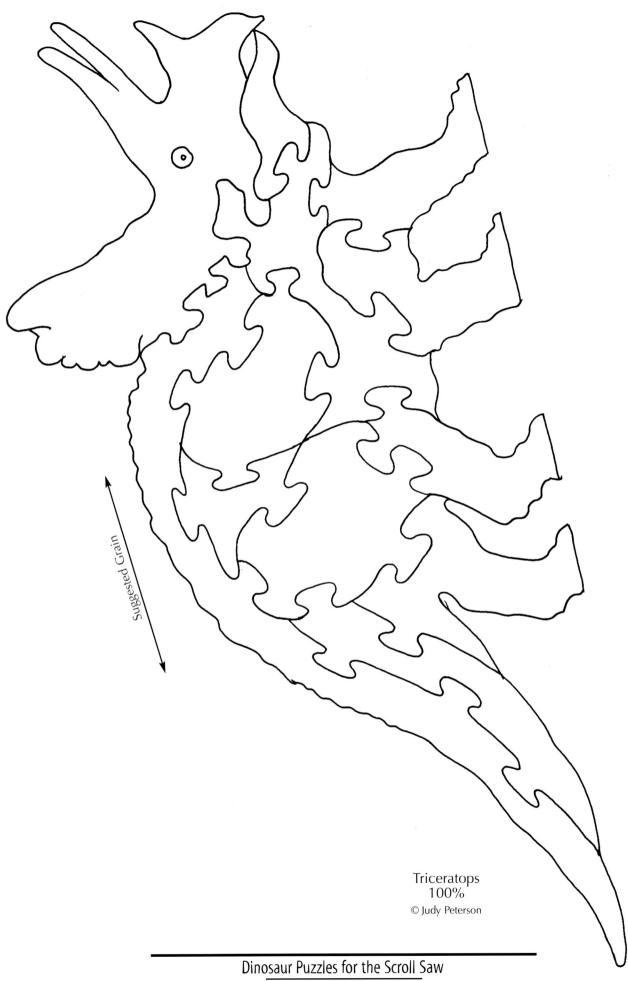

Suggested Grain

Triceratops
100%

© Judy Peterson

Triceratops

Triceratops (Three Horned Face) is a Ceratopsian from the
Cretaceous Age. This plant eater was found in North America and
grew to be about 25 feet long and 9 feet tall.
(Cut from Goncalo Alves.)

Suggested Grain

Pachyrhinosaur
100%
© Judy Peterson

Dinosaur Puzzles for the Scroll Saw

38

Pachyrhinosaur

Advanced

Pachyrhinosaur (Thick-Nosed Lizard) was a plant eater found in North America during the Cretaceous Age. This Ceratopsian grew to about 20 feet long and four tons. (Cut from cherry.)

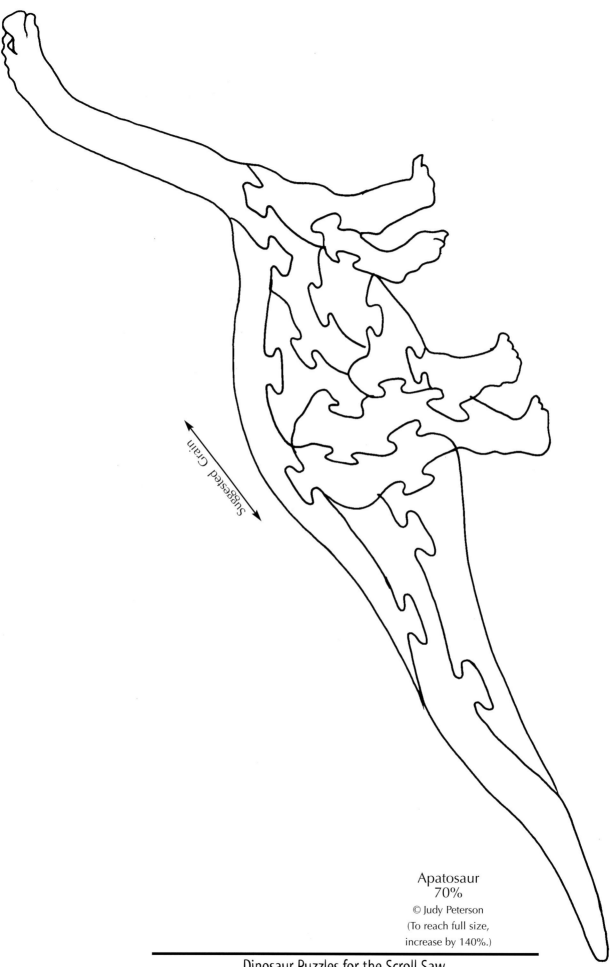

Apatosaur
70%
© Judy Peterson
(To reach full size,
increase by 140%.)

Suggested Grain

Apatosaur

Apatosaur (Deceptive Lizard) was formerly called Brontosaur. A Sauropod of the Jurassic Age, this animal was found in North America and Europe. It ate plants and grew to be about 75 feet long, 15 feet tall and 30 tons. (Cut from redgum.)

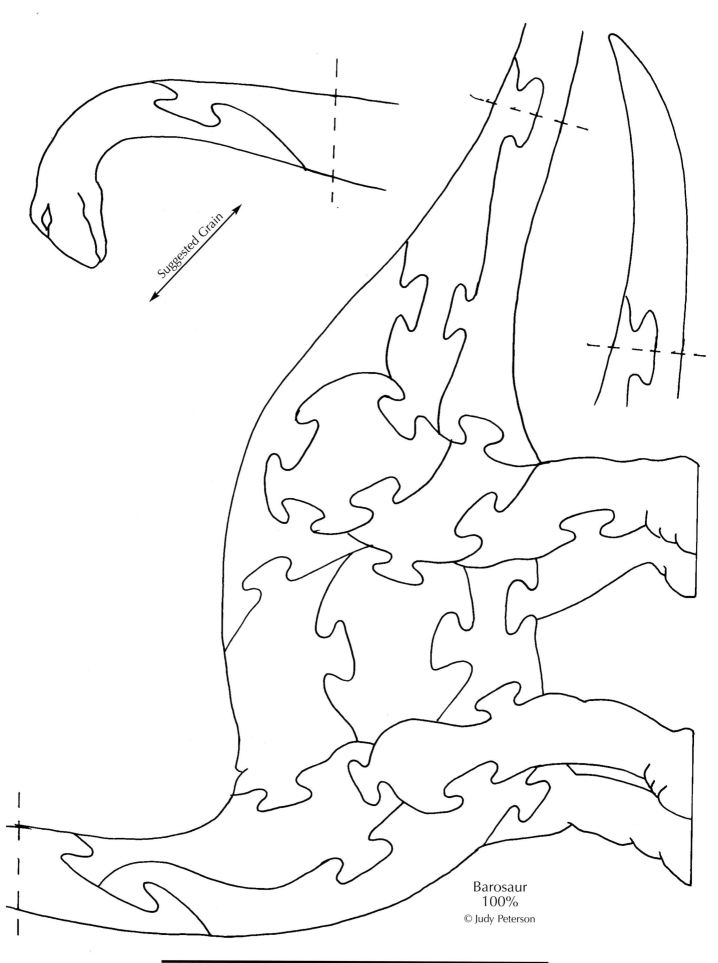

Suggested Grain

Barosaur
100%

© Judy Peterson

Barosaur

Barosaur (Heavy Lizard) was the longest Sauropod, measuring
nearly 90 feet long. This plant eater was found in North America
and Africa during the Jurassic Age. (Cut from Makore.)

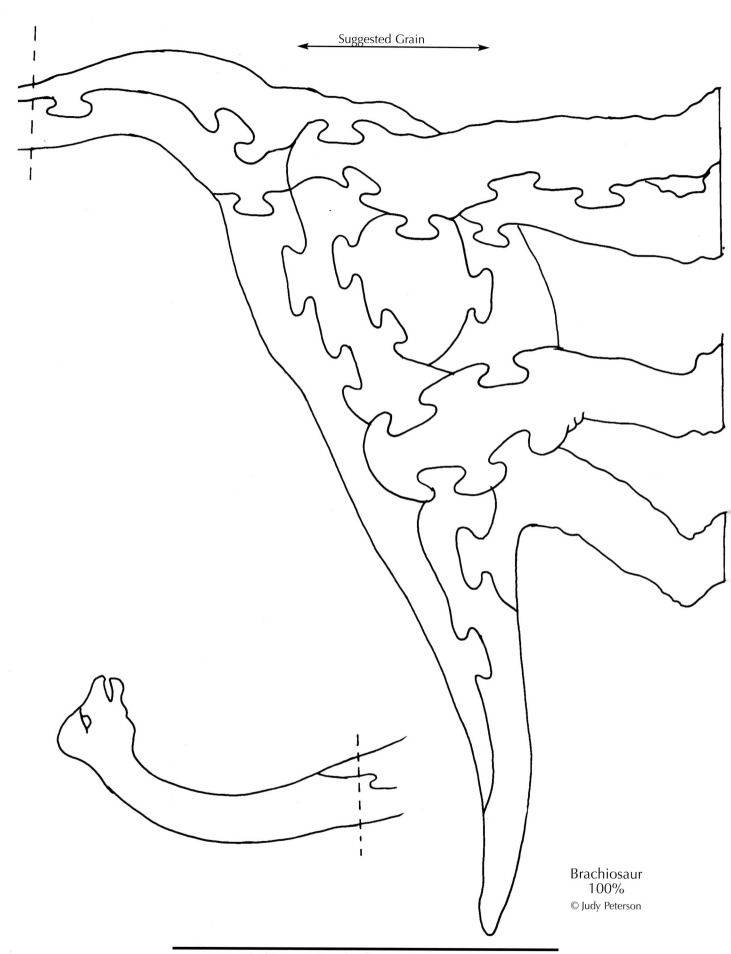

Suggested Grain

Brachiosaur
100%
© Judy Peterson

Dinosaur Puzzles for the Scroll Saw

44

Brachiosaur

Brachiosaur (Arm Lizard) stood taller than a four-story building. This plant-eating Sauropod from the Jurassic Age was found in North America, Europe and Africa. It grew to about 85 feet long, 40 feet tall and weighed 70 to 80 tons. (Cut from cherry.)

Suggested Grain

Ichthyosaur
100%
© Judy Peterson

Ichthyosaur

Ichthyosaur (Fish Lizard) was a marine reptile of the Triassic, Jurassic and Cretaceous Ages. A fish-eater, it was found in North America, South America and Europe. (Cut from cherry.)

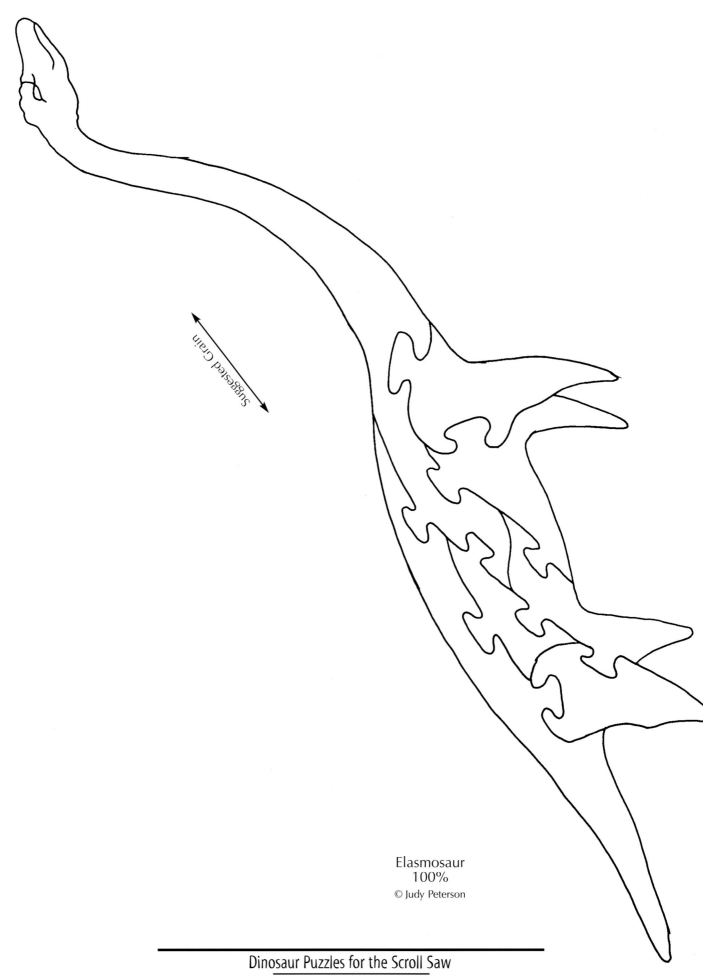

Suggested Grain

Elasmosaur
100%
© Judy Peterson

Elasmosaur

Elasmosaur (Thin-Plated Lizard) ate fish and lived during the Cretaceous Age. A marine reptile, it was found in North America and measured about 43 feet long. (Cut from walnut.)

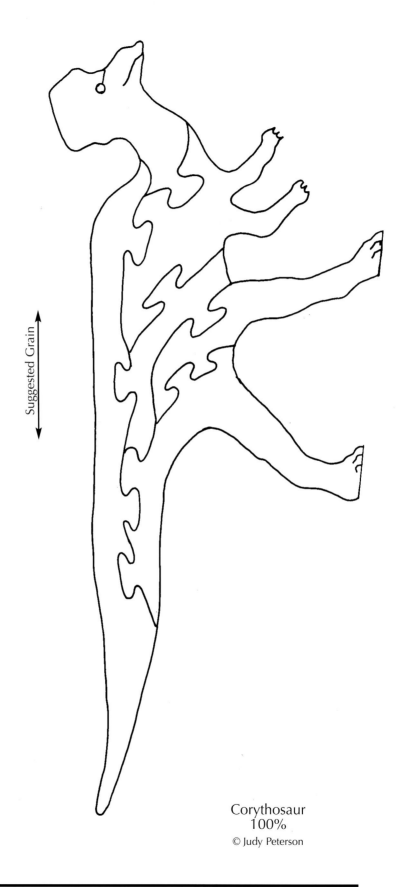

Suggested Grain

Corythosaur
100%

© Judy Peterson

Corythosaur

Corythosaur (Helmet Lizard) was a Hadrosaur of the Cretaceous Age. This plant eater was found in North America and measured about 30 feet long. (Cut from Chakte Kok.)

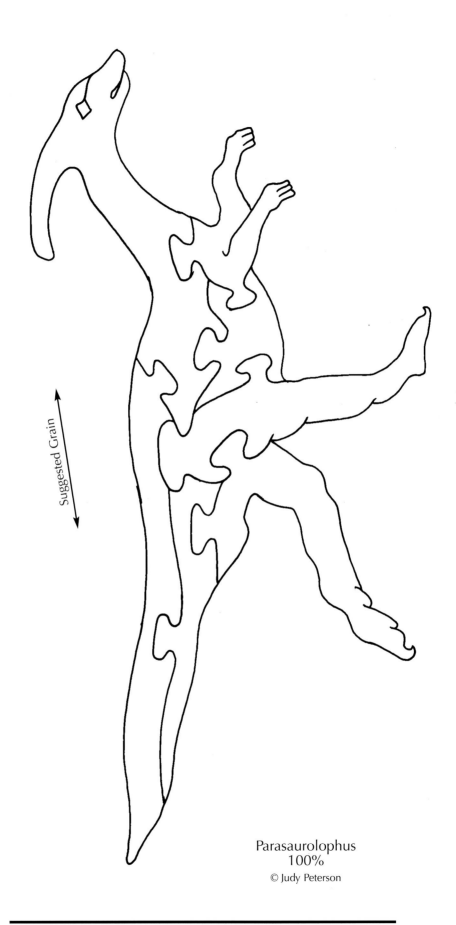

Suggested Grain

Parasaurolophus
100%

© Judy Peterson

Parasaurolophus

Parasaurolophus (Similar Crested Lizard) was a Hadrosaur that
lived in North America during the Cretaceous Age. A plant eater,
it measured about 30 feet long and 16 feet tall with a crest about
5 feet long. (Cut from walnut.)

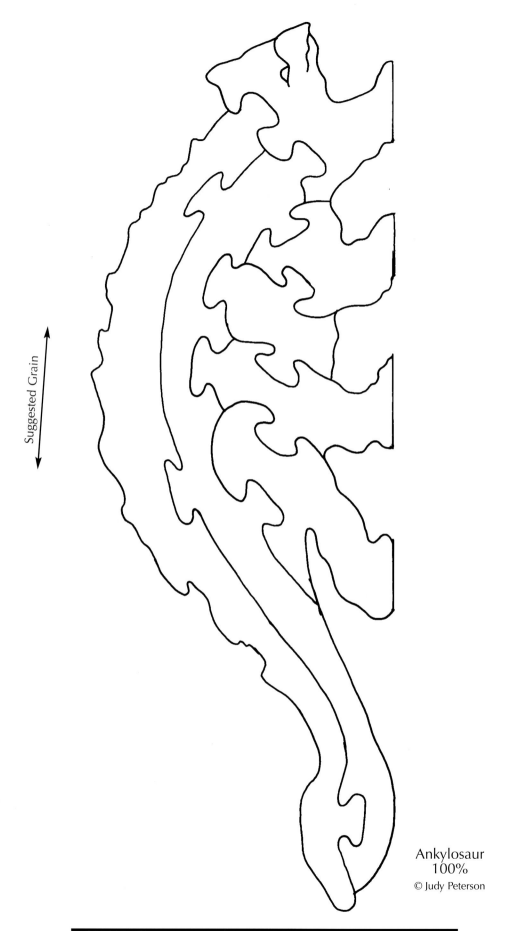

Suggested Grain

Ankylosaur
100%

© Judy Peterson

Ankylosaur

Ankylosaur (Armored Lizard) was found in North America during the Cretaceous Age. It ate plants and grew to about 25 feet long, 6 feet wide and 4 feet tall. (Cut from walnut.)

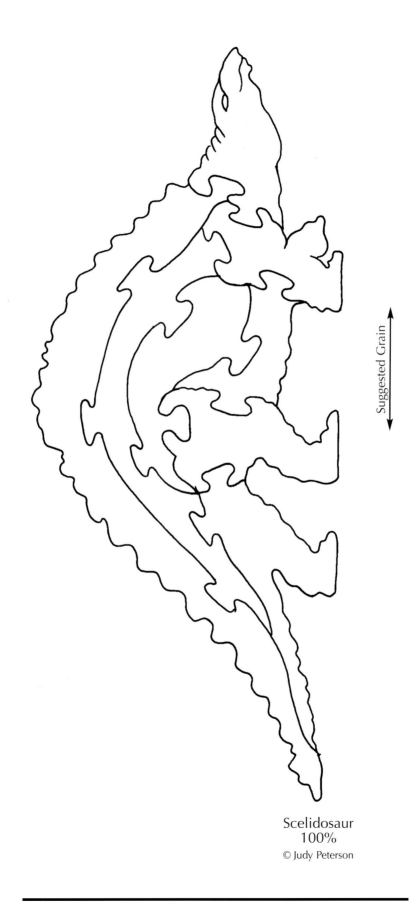

Scelidosaur
100%

© Judy Peterson

Suggested Grain

Scelidosaur

Scelidosaur (Ribbed Lizard) was an Ankylosaurid from the
Jurassic Age. This plant eater was found in England and
measured about 12 feet long. (Cut from Maca.)

Suggested Grain

Stegosaur
100%

© Judy Peterson

Dinosaur Puzzles for the Scroll Saw

Stegosaur

Stegosaur (Plated Lizard) lived in North America and Europe during the Jurassic Age. It was a plant eater that grew to about 25 feet long and 11 feet tall at the hip. (Cut from cherry.)

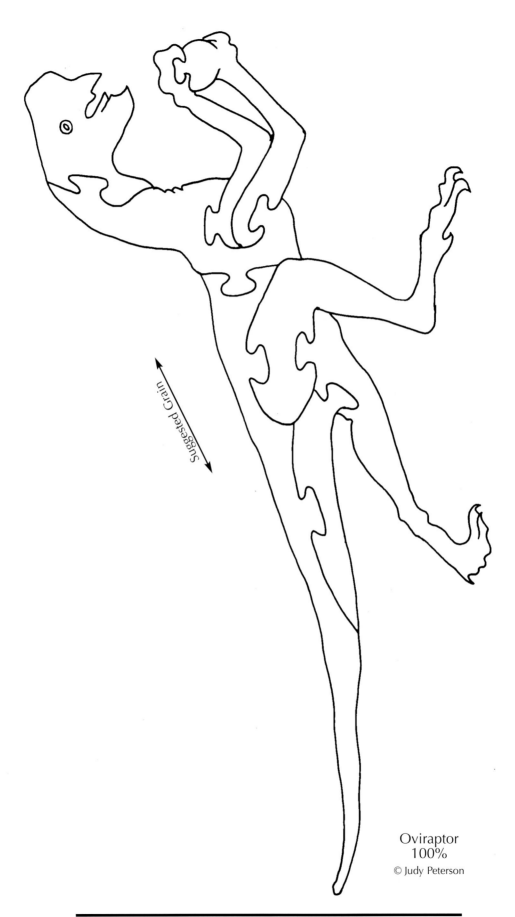

Suggested Grain

Oviraptor
100%
© Judy Peterson

Oviraptor

Advanced

Oviraptor (Egg Stealer) was one of the most peculiar-looking dinosaurs. This Theropod from the Cretaceous Age was called "egg stealer" because it was found with a nest of eggs. It ate both meat and plants and grew to about 5 feet long. (Cut from cherry.)

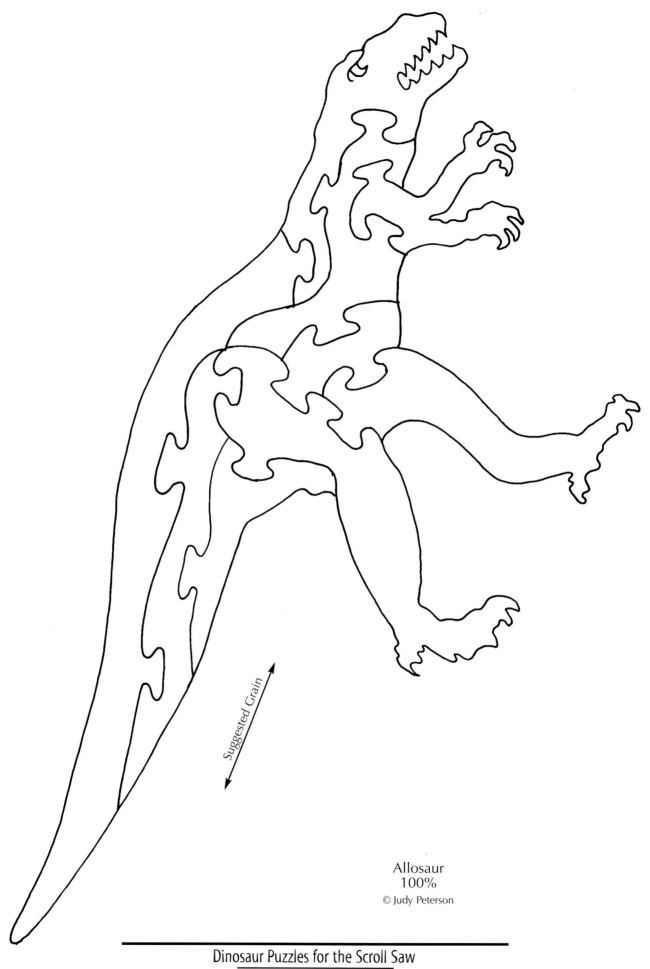

Suggested Grain

Allosaur
100%

© Judy Peterson

Allosaur

Allosaur (Different Lizard) was a Therapod from the Jurassic Age.
This meat eater was found in North America, Africa and Asia. It
measured about 35 to 45 feet long and weighed about 4 tons.
(Cut from cherry.)

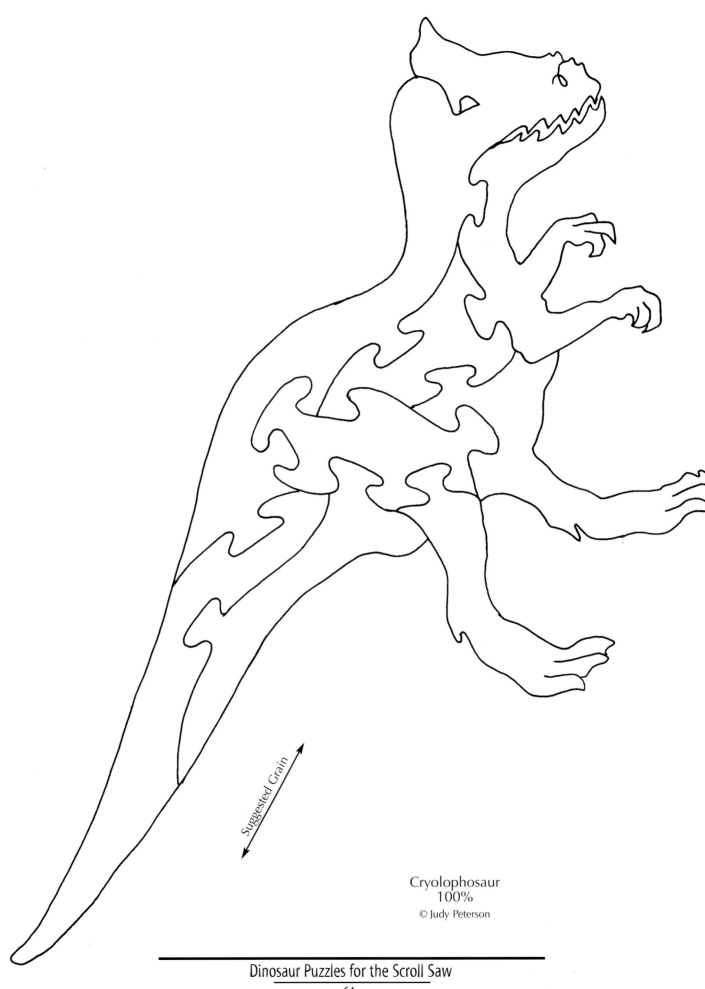

Cryolophosaur
100%

© Judy Peterson

Suggested Grain

Dinosaur Puzzles for the Scroll Saw

64

Cryolophosaur

Cryolophosaur (Frozen-Crested Lizard) was found in Antarctica.
This meat eater was about 24 feet long and lived in the
Early Jurassic Age. (Cut from walnut.)

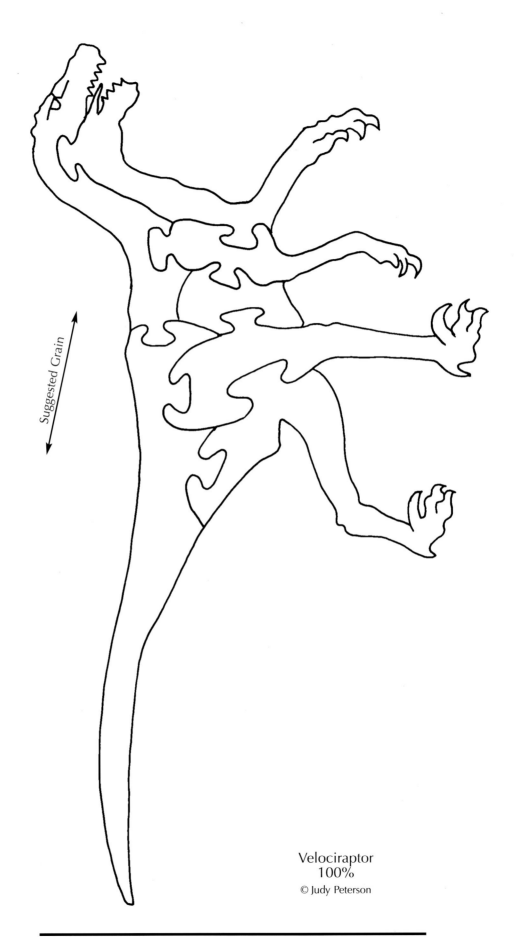

Suggested Grain

Velociraptor
100%
© Judy Peterson

Velociraptor

Velociraptor (Speedy Robber) was a small, very fast dinosaur. This Theropod from the Cretaceous Age was about 6 feet long and probably hunted in packs. (Cut from walnut.)

Maiasaur

Diorama

This puzzle is based on the site in Montana where the remains of several Maiasaur dinosaurs were found—complete with babies. The nest was about seven feet wide. This Hadrosaur's name means Good Mother Lizard. The adults were plant eaters that grew to nearly 30 feet long. (Cut from walnut.)

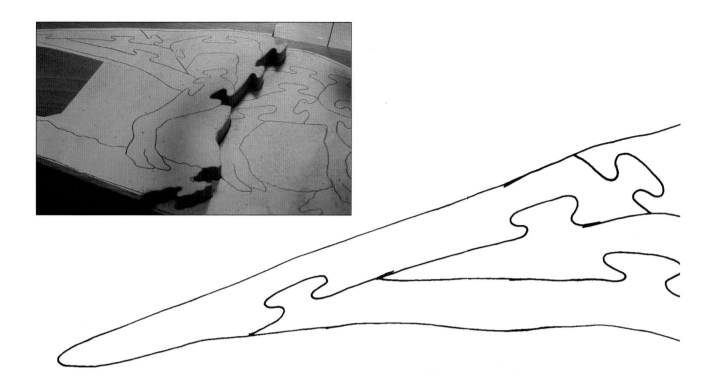

Cutting the Maiasaur's babies

First, drill the holes that represent the babies' eyes. Because of the length of this puzzle, segment the puzzle down the center (see photo above), then cut the three babies free. Turn each into twins as follows: Lay one baby on its back. Starting at the head, slice it in half. With the two babies that do not lay flat on the saw table, you'll need to compensate. When you get to the hind leg, tip the head up and the tail down while you slice. Support the tail on the saw table until you finish the cut.

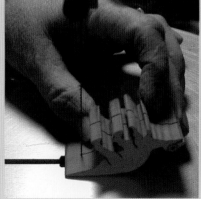

Cutting Large Patterns

Large patterns don't have to be difficult to cut. To handle In the Cretaceous on page 72, cut the puzzle in half down the center along the tall Cycad. Then cut along the T-Rex's back to free the top and the bottom on one half. Cut the Cycad free. Now cut along the back of the Lambeosaur. This results in four pieces of manageable sizes plus the tall Cycad.

Creative Keys

Key shapes can be varied almost infinitely as long as you remember to get a little material on both sides of the head. The dioramas on pages 68 and 72 are perfect examples of creative keys. The keys that hold the mountains together are the conifer trees. The major key is the tall Cycad, a palm tree-shaped piece that holds the two sections of the puzzle together.

These keys played a major part in the design of In the Cretaceous (page 72). I positioned the Lambeosaur and the T-Rex first, then designed the puzzle cuts. Around them I built the landscape with mountains for back ground and a ground line for the dinosaurs to stand on. Then I placed Conifers and Cycads (plants that lived at that time) in locations where they could act as keys. The tall Cycad made an ideal central element with roots and leaves forming keys.

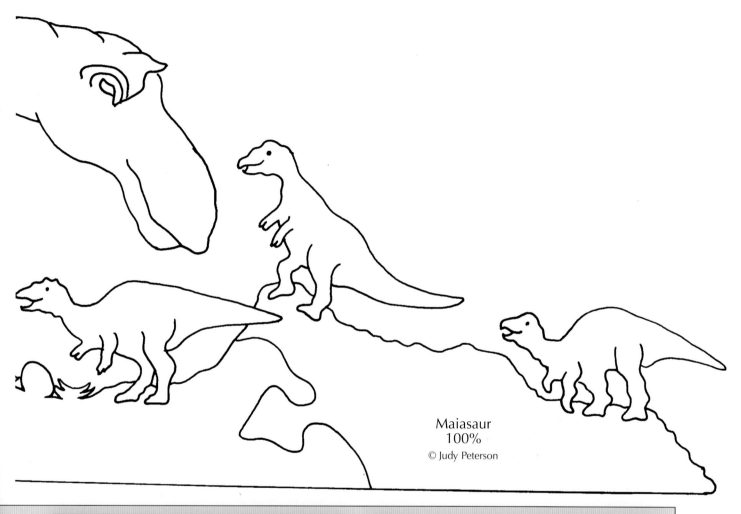

Maiasaur
100%
© Judy Peterson

Dinosaur Puzzles for the Scroll Saw

In the Cretaceous

"In the Cretaceous" shows a Tyrannosaurus Rex about to attack its prey, a plant-eating Lambeosaur. Except for the Conifer trees, which looked pretty much like they do today, all the other plants are Cycads. All of these life forms lived in the Late Cretaceous Era, 65 to 100 million years ago. (Cut from Baltic birch and cherry.)

Cut the backerboard from Baltic birch or any thin plywood. Cut the stands from scrap puzzle wood. The exterior of the stands can be any shape you like. The bottom of the stands should be ½-inch thick for strength. The interior dimension should be the sum of the widths of your puzzle board plus your backer board plus a hair's width for clearance.

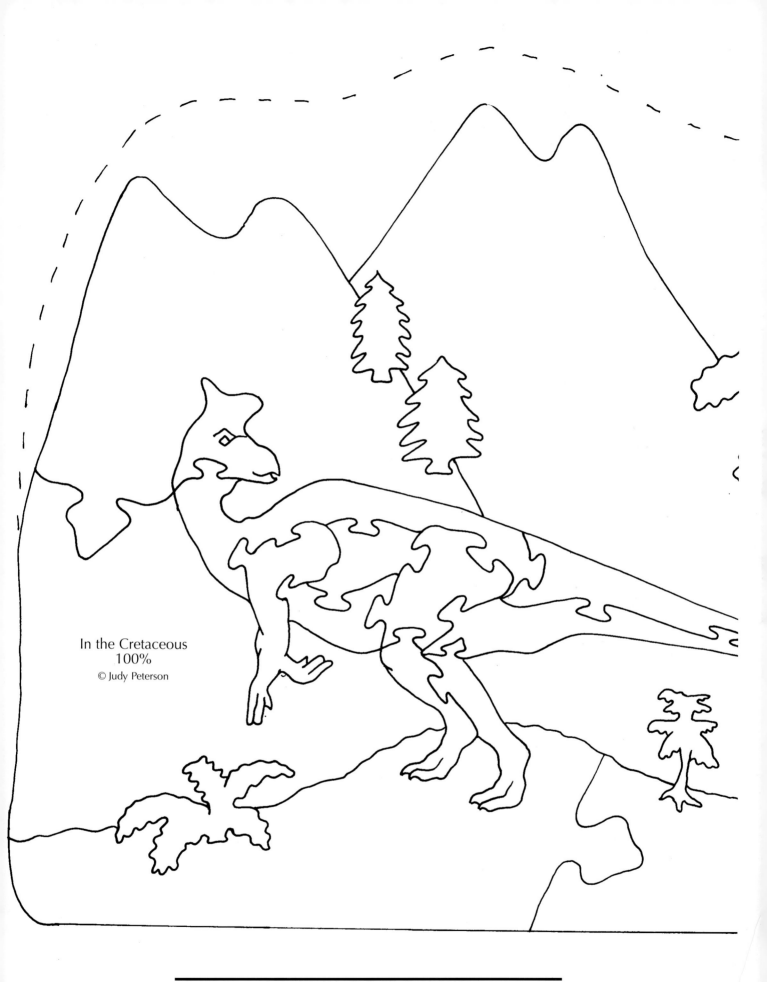

In the Cretaceous
100%
© Judy Peterson

Stand (cut four)

Dashed line
represents the
backerboard

Dinosaur Puzzles for the Scroll Saw

More Great Project Books from Fox Chapel Publishing